Lunch Fun!

Best 50 Bento Recipes for Kids

BY

Julia Chiles

OOOOOOOOOOOOOOOOOOOOOOOOOOOOOOOOOOOOOOO

D0830172

License Notes

OOOOOOOOOOOOOOOOOOOOOOOOOOOOOOOOOOOOOOOO

Table of Contents

Introduction

Looking for some great bento kids lunch recipes? You need, Lunch Fun! 50 Bento Recipes for Kids! A mix of fun and healthy bento recipes to take lunch to the next level. Delicious proteins, fruits and veggies, homemade treats, trail mixes, and novel protein bars. Unforgettable bento fun!

A Few Tips for Bento Kids

1) Leftovers are a bento boxes' best friend.

2) Imagination goes a long way with children.

3) For kids' lunch is as a social event. Keep it light and fun!

4) Colorful foods and creative utensils go a long way with all kids, even stubborn and picky eaters!

5) Turn lunch time into fun time!

6) Rubber skewers (kid safe) are available online.

Italian Chicken Quinoa

Great for leftover chicken! Makes 1 bento box

Ingredients:

- 1 small box of raisins
- 3-5 segments orange, tangerine, etc.
- 1 container of whole grain O's (such as Cheerios)
- 2 tbsp canned chicken, drained, washed
- ¼ cup quinoa
- 1/3 tsp Italian seasoning
- 1 tbsp diced scallions -or- julienned onions (optional)

Instructions:

Mix canned chicken, quinoa, Italian seasoning, and onions.

Place in Italian chicken quinoa in 1st compartment.

Place raisins in 2nd compartment.

Place oranges/tangerines in 3rd compartment.

Place cereal in 4th compartment.

Lettuce Wraps and Dried Apple Chips

Also, great with diced ham. Males 1 bento box.

Ingredients:

- ¼ can chicken, washed drained
- ½ cup mayonnaise
- 1/3 tsp salt free onion and herb
- 2-3 lettuce leaves
- 1 tbsp dried cranberries
- ½-2/3 tbsp crushed walnuts
- 1 tbsp chocolate chips or candy-coated chocolate candies (such as MMs)
- 1 tbsp peanut butter chips
- 5 wheat squares
- 5 dried apple chips

Instructions:

Mix chicken, mayonnaise, seasoning.

Fill each leaf with 1 spoonful of chicken salad, roll, and seal by dipping your finger in water then running it down the edge. Place in 1st compartment.

Mix cranberries, crushed walnuts, chips/candies, peanut butter chips. Place in 2nd compartment.

Place wheat squares in 3rd compartment.

Place apple chips in 4th compartment.

Cherry Tomatoes Blueberry Pancakes

There are lots of great gluten free, natural, and organic options! Makes 1 bento box.

Ingredients:

- 5-7 carrot sticks
- 1-2 hardboiled eggs, sliced
- 5-7 cherry tomatoes
- 2-3 mini blueberry pancakes or waffles cut into triangles

Instructions:

Place carrots in 1st compartment.

Place egg slices in 2nd compartment.

Place cherry tomatoes in 3rd compartment.

Place pancakes/waffles in 4th compartment.

Mozzarella Pizza Bagels

Want more protein? Spread some peanut butter on the celery! Makes 1 bento box.

Ingredients:

- 5-8 colorful bell peppers or carrots.
- 5-8 sticks of celery
- 1 small round or stick of mozzarella cheese (such as Baby Bell)
- 2-3 pizza bagels

Instructions:

Wash bell peppers, carrots, and celery very well.

Place peppers/carrots in 1st compartment.

Place celery sticks. In 2nd compartment.

Place cheese in 3rd compartment.

Place pizza bagels in 4th compartment.

P.B. Toast Pita Chips

For an extra treat sprinkle some cinnamon into the peanut
butter. Makes 1 bento box

Ingredients:

- 2 slices of bread
- Peanut butter
- ½ cup low sodium pita chips
- 3-4 chocolate sandwich cookies
- 4-7 broccoli trees
- 1 container melted cheddar cheese or Italian dressing

Instructions:

Make toast, spread on peanut butter, cut in half, and place in corresponding compartment.

Place chips in 2nd compartment (if desired, add some hummus).

Place cookies in 3rd compartment.

Place broccoli trees and container of sauce in 4th compartment.

Homemade Crispy Bars and Fish Sticks

Homemade crispy bars are really protein bars in disguise!
Makes 1 bento box.

Ingredients:

- 4-5 low sodium fish sticks
- 1-2 homemade crispy bars*
- 4-5 pieces of edamame
- 4-5 graham shaped teddy bears or dog bones (Teddy Grahams Scooby Snacks)

Instructions:

Place fish sticks 1st compartment.

Place crispy bars in 2nd compartment.

Place edamame in 3rd compartment

Place graham treats in 4th compartment.

*Homemade Crispy Bars

Ingredients:

- 1 bag mini marshmallows
- 1 stick sweet cream butter
- 5-5 ½ cups crispy rice cereal
- ¼ cup peanut butter protein powder
- ¼ cup cocoa powder
- 1 tbsp cinnamon
- 2 tbsp honey (optional)
- 1 tub colorful frosting (i.e.- orange, blue, purple)
- Sprinkles

Instructions:

Makes 9x11 dish

In a small pot let stick of butter melt halfway then stir in marshmallows.

Over a 20-30-minute period and oscillating heat, let meld together, stirring constantly until smooth.

In a large bowl combine cereal, peanut butter powder, cocoa powder, and cinnamon.

Pour butter/marshmallow mixture over cereal and toss.

Line dish with parchment paper.

Spread mixture evenly into dish.

Spread on frosting and sprinkles.

Keep covered or stored in airtight container and will keep 1 week.

Quesadillas and Coconut Bars

Ingredients:

- 2-4 triangles cheese quesadilla
- 1-2 coconut bars*
- 5-8 tortilla chips
- 1 container salsa
- 4-5 dried pineapple chips

Instructions:

Place quesadilla triangles in 1st compartment.

Place coconut bars in 2nd compartment.

Place chips and container of salsa in 3rd compartment

Place pineapple chips in 4th compartment

Coconut Bars

Ingredients:

- 1/3 cup + 2 tbsp pure maple syrup
- 2 tbsp + 2 tsp coconut oil
- ¼ tsp vanilla (substitute with honey)
- 1 tbsp cinnamon
- 2/3 tsp nutmeg
- 1 tsp cocoa powder
- 5-6 cups old-fashion oats

Instructions:

In a microwavable safe bowl, melt coconut oil and maple syrup together in 30 second increments.

Stir until smooth, add vanilla, incorporate well but do not over stir.

In a large bowl combine oats, cinnamon, cocoa powder, and nutmeg.

Pour maple syrup/coconut oil mixture over the oats. Stir well.

Line baking tray with parchment paper.

Spread mixture out evenly on tray.

Bake 20 minutes.

Flip granola bake another 15 minutes.

Stored in airtight container will keep up to 2 weeks.

Dyno-Ham-a-Sandwich

Find tons of creative sandwich cutters online! Makes 1 bento box.

Ingredients:

- Dino shaped ham sandwich
- 5 cheese cubes
- 2 chocolate chip cookies
- 5-10 veggie chips

Instructions:

Place sandwich in 1st compartment.

Place cheese cubes in 2nd compartment.

Place cookies in 3rd compartment.

Place veggie chips in 4th compartment.

Baked Gluten Free Chicken Nuggets

Applesauce

Buy them frozen or use the recipe below! Makes 1 bento box.

Ingredients:

- 4-5 Baked Gluten Free Chicken Nuggets*
- 1 container sugar-free applesauce
- 5-10 veggie chips
- 1 package gummy snack fruit chews

Instructions:

Place chicken nuggets in 1st compartment.

Place applesauce in 2nd compartment.

Place veggie chips in 3rd compartment

Place fruit chews in 4th compartment

Gluten Free Baked Chicken Nuggets

Ingredients:

- 1 boneless, skinless chicken breasts cut into nuggets
- 2 large eggs
- 1 cup gluten friendly all-purpose flour
  - 1 cup gluten free breadcrumbs

Instructions:

Preheat oven to 400-425 and prepare baking tray by lining with aluminum foil.

Set up breading station: fill one bowl with beaten eggs, one with all-purpose flour, one will gluten free breadcrumbs.

Coat chicken pieces with egg, then coat pieces with all-purpose flour, and finally into gluten free breadcrumbs.

Place on baking tray and cook 30 minutes.

Broccoli Slaw Crackers

Broccoli slaw is great for tailoring! Makes 1 bento box.

Ingredients:

- 1 cup broccoli slaw mix
- ½ - 2/3 cup ham, large diced
- 1 tbsp crushed walnuts -or- slivered almonds (optional)
- 1 small container of mild Italian dressing or extra virgin olive oil with parsley and lemon juice
- 5-8 cherry tomatoes
- 5-8 slices red pepper
- 5 graham crackers

Instructions:

Combine broccoli slaw, ham, nuts.

Place slaw and container of dressing, in 1st compartment.

Place cherry tomatoes in 2nd compartment.

Place red pepper sticks in 3rd compartment.

Place graham crackers in 4th compartment.

Dried Apricots Peanut Butter Graham Crackers

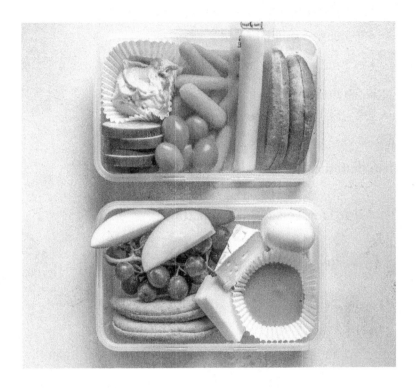

Peanut butter is a great source of protein! Makes 1 box.

Ingredients:

- 1/4 cup dried apricots
- 1 tbsp raisins
- 5 carrot sticks
- 5 red or purple seedless grapes
- 6 graham crackers
- Peanut butter

Instructions:

Place dried apricots in 1st compartment.

Place raisins in 2nd compartment.

Place carrot sticks in 3rd compartment.

Place peanut butter graham crackers in 4th compartment.

Hot Dogs and Pretzels

Don't forget the ketchup! Makes 1 bento box.

Ingredients:

- 1 hot dog, sliced
- 5 apple slices
- 5 cheese cubes
- 5 mini pretzels

Instructions:

Place hot dog slices in 1st compartment.

Place apple slices in 2nd compartment.

Place cheese cubes in 3rd compartment.

Place strawberries in 4th compartment.

Chocolate Hazelnut Waffles Bento

Mini rice cakes work too! Makes 1 bento box.

Ingredients:

- 2-3 mini waffles
- 1 tbsp chocolate hazelnut spread
- ¼ cup pretzels
- ¼ cup dried cranberries
- 5 cheese cubes

Instructions:

Spread chocolate hazelnut spread on mini waffles and place in 1st compartment.

Place pretzels in 1st compartment.

Place dried cranberries in 2nd compartment.

Place carrot sticks in 3rd compartment.

Place cheese cubes in 4th compartment.

P.B.S.J

Peanut butter candies, such as Reese's Piece's work too!
Makes 1 bento box.

Ingredients:

- Peanut butter sandwich with strawberry jelly cut as heart or star
- 1-2 tbsp chocolate candies (such as MMs)
- ¼ cup blueberries
- 5-7 pieces of edamame

Instructions:

Place sandwich in 1st compartment.

Place candies in 2nd compartment.

Place blueberries in 3rd compartment.

Place edamame in 4th compartment.

Pancake Sandwiches Cheesy Crackers

Try blueberry pancakes! Makes 1 bento box.

Ingredients:

- 2 silver dollar pancakes
- 1 tbsp cream cheese (softened)
- 1 tsp cinnamon
- 1 tsp maple syrup
- 5 cheese crackers (such as Ritz)
- 5 carrot sticks
- 4 Graham cracker teddy bears or dog bones (such as Teddy Grahams and Scooby Snacks)

Instructions:

Cream cheese should be a little bit looser than typical frosting; in microwave safe dish melt in 10 second intervals.

Mix cream cheese, cinnamon, syrup then spread on pancakes.

Place crackers in 2nd compartment.

Place carrot sticks in 3rd compartment.

Place graham treats in 4th compartment.

Cheesy Triangles

Put some salsa in that quesadilla! Makes 1 bento box.

Ingredients:

- 1 cheese quesadilla cut into 4 or 8 triangles.
- 5 veggie chips
- 5 trees of broccoli
- 5 red pepper sticks
- 1 small container of ranch dressing

Instructions:

Place quesadilla triangles in 1st compartment.

Place veggie chips in 2nd compartment.

Place broccoli in 3rd compartment.

Place pepper sticks along with container of ranch dressing in 4th compartment.

Melon Salad and Sweet Peppers

Use seasonal melons! Makes 1 bento box.

Ingredients:

- 2-3 cubes of watermelon
- 2-3 cubes of cantaloupe
- 2-3 green seedless grapes
- 3-5 cheese cubes
- 5 sweet peppers
- 1 crispy rice treat (a.k.a. Rice Krispy Treat)

Instructions:

Mix watermelon, cantaloupe and grapes.

Place in first compartment.

Place cheese cubes in 2nd compartment.

Place sweet peppers 3rd compartment.

Place crispy rice treat in 4th compartment.

Strawberry Sandwiches and Crackers

Substitute mini waffles for mini pancakes! Makes 1 bento box.

Ingredients:

- 4 mini pancakes (frozen is fine)
- 1-2 tbsp strawberry flavored cream cheese
- 1 crispy treat cut into ½ - 2/3-inch cubes (a.k.a. rice crispy treats)
- 3-5 butter crackers or cheese crackers
- 1 fruit cup

Instructions:

Layout 2 mini pancakes, spread strawberry cream cheese on them, top with remaining 2 pancakes then place in first compartment.

Place crispy rice treat in 2nd compartment.

Place crackers 3rd compartment.

Place fruit cup in 4th compartment.

Strawberry Hearts and Ants on Logs

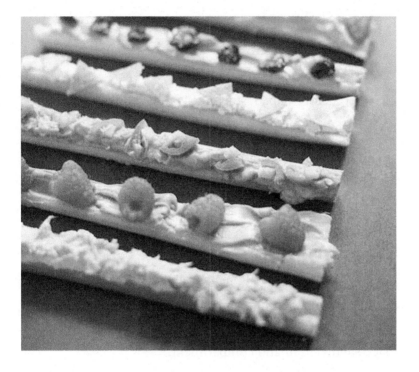

Try organic peanut butters! Makes 1 bento box.

Ingredients:

- 5 celery sticks
- 1 cup peanut butter
- 25-30 raisins
- 1 heart shaped strawberry jelly and peanut butter sandwich
- 2-3 large marshmallows
- 2-3 graham crackers

Instructions:

Layout celery sticks fill with peanut butter, top with 4-6 raisins, and place in first compartment.

Place sandwich in 2nd compartment.

Place marshmallows in 3rd compartment.

Place graham crackers in 4th compartment.

Avocado Toast with Cinnamon Apple Slices

Throw in some grape tomatoes! Makes 1 bento box.

Ingredients:

- 1 slice toasted bread
- 1/3 cup avocado puree
- 1 tub yogurt
- 1 granola bar
- 3-4 cinnamon apple slices

Instructions:

Place avocado toast in 1st compartment.

Place yogurt in 2nd compartment.

Place granola bar in 3rd compartment.

Place apple slices in 4th compartment.

Grilled Cheese and Apple Slices

Try dipping the grilled cheese in honey! Makes 1 bento box.

Ingredients:

- 1 grilled cheese
- 2-3 graham crackers
- 1 pudding snack pack
- 5 apple slices
- 1 container honey

Instructions:

Place grilled cheese in 1st compartment.

Place graham crackers in 2nd compartment.

Place pudding in 3rd compartment.

Place in apple slices in 4th compartment with container of honey.

Pizza Rounds and Fruit Cocktail

Use up leftover biscuits! Makes 1 bento box.

Ingredients:

- 2 biscuits
- ½ cup pizza sauce
- 1 cup shredded mozzarella or pizza cheese
- 1/3 cup mini pepperoni (optional)
- 2 1 cup of fruit cocktail
- 3 1/3 cup dried cranberries
- 4 3-4 sandwich cookies

Instructions:

Open biscuits, spread all halves with sauce, top with cheese and all desired toppings, then put under broiler 3-4 minutes or until cheese melts then place in first compartment.

Place fruit cocktail in 2nd compartment.

Place dried cranberries in 3rd compartment.

Place cookies in 4th compartment.

Fruit Salad and Granola Bites

Great for seasonal fruits and veggies! Makes 1 bento box.

Ingredients:

- 1 1/3 cup dried pomegranates or cranberries
- 2-3 segments pineapples
- 2-3 segments tangerine
- 2-3 cherries
- 1 granola bar cut into ½ -1-inch pieces
- 1 fun shaped peanut butter sandwich with chocolate hazelnut spread
- ½ string cheese

Instructions:

Combine pomegranates or cranberries, pineapples, tangerines, and cherries and place in first compartment.

Place granola bites in 2nd compartment.

Place sandwich in 3rd compartment.

Place ½ string cheese in 4th compartment.

Lettuce Roll and Pears

Try various deli meats! Makes 1 bento box.

Ingredients:

- 2 large lettuce leaf
- 4 slices thin deli turkey
- 1/3 -1/2 tbsp mayonnaise or mustard
- 3-4 apple slices
- 2-4 pears
- 3-4 pretzels

Instructions:

Layout lettuce leaves, spread on mayonnaise/mustard, top with turkey, roll, and place in first compartment.

Layout apples in 2nd compartment.

Place pretzels in 3rd compartment.

Place pears in 4th compartment.

Hot Dogs and Raisins

Don't forget the ketchup! Makes 1 bento box.

Ingredients:

- 2-3 hot dog, sliced
- 1/2 banana
- 1 box of raisins
- 1 tub yogurt

Instructions:

Place sliced hot dogs in first compartment.

Place ½ banana in 2nd compartment.

Place box of raisins in 3rd compartment.

Place yogurt in 4th compartment.

Links and Sticks

Prosciutto wrapped in cheese is another great idea! Makes 1 bento box.

Ingredients:

- 2-3 chicken sausages
- 5 broccoli trees and container of ranch dressing
- 5-8 bell pepper sticks
- 1 pudding snack pack

Instructions:

In skillet cook sausage links as directed, cut into 1-inch long pieces, place in first compartment.

Place carrot sticks in 2nd compartment along with container of ranch dressing.

Place bell pepper sticks in 3rd compartment.

Place pudding snack pack in 4th compartment.

Bacon, Eggs, and Pancakes

Breakfast is good any time of day! Makes 1 bento box.

Ingredients:

- 3-4 silver dollar blueberry pancakes
- 1 hardboiled egg, sliced
- 1 slice of bacon, halved
- ½ cup strawberries, washed

Instructions:

Place pancakes in 1st compartment.

Place hardboiled egg and in 2nd compartment.

Place bacon, halved, in 3rd compartment.

Place strawberries in 4th compartment.

Fill one compartment with blueberries.

Ham and Cheese Crackers

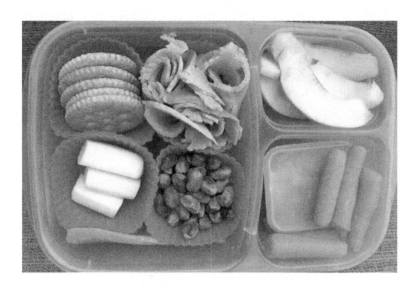

Make lunch fun again! Makes 1 bento box.

Ingredients:

- 5 or 10 butter crackers*
- 5 pieces of thin ham*
- 5 pieces of Colby jack*
- 5 veggie straws
- 5 seedless grapes
- 2-3 cookies

Instructions:

Cut ham and cheese to fit on top of crackers then place in 1st compartment

Place veggie straws in 2nd compartments.

Place grapes in 3rd compartment.

Place cookies in 4th compartment.

Tuna Salad and Cookies

Great protein box. Makes 1 bento box.

Ingredients:

- 1 pouch organic/mercury free tuna salad
- 5-7 saltines
- 5-7 celery sticks
- 2-3 cookies

Instructions:

Place tuna in first compartment.

Place saltines in 2nd compartment.

Place celery sticks in 3rd compartment.

Place cookies in 4th compartment.

Zoodles and O's

Try sweet potato spirals or butternut squash! Makes 1 bento box.

Ingredients:

- 1/2 cup zucchini noodles
- 3-5 grape tomatoes
- 2 tbsp low sodium Italian dressing
- 1/3 cup o shaped cereal (for example, Cheerio's)
- 1/2 string cheese
- 5-10 goldfish

Instructions:

Mix zucchini noodles and grape tomatoes then place in 1st compartment.

Place cereal in 2nd compartment.

Place ½ string cheese in 3rd compartment.

Place goldfish in 4th compartment.

Sandwich Cutouts and Cheesy Broccoli

Switch out the container of cheese for ranch dressing sometimes! Makes 1 bento box.

Ingredients:

- 1 peanut butter and jelly sandwich
- Favorite cookie cutter shape/shapes
- 1/3 cup goldfish
- 4-5 bell pepper sticks
- 5 broccoli trees
- 1 container cheese

Instructions:

Place sandwich cutouts in 1st compartment.

Place goldfish in 2nd compartment.

Place broccoli tress and cheese in 3rd compartment.

Place bell pepper sticks in 4th compartment.

Quinoa and Quesadilla

Sprinkle some chili powder in the quesadilla for added flavor! Makes 1 bento box.

Ingredients:

- 1 triangles cheese quesadilla
- 2 ½ cup of quinoa
- 1 tbsp pine nuts or crushed walnuts (optional)
- 3 1 pack fruit chews
- 4 celery sticks

Instructions:

Place triangles in 1st compartment.

Place quinoa in 2nd compartment.

Place fruit chews in 3rd compartment.

Place celery sticks in 4th compartment.

Veggies and Beans

Try various types of beans! Makes 1 bento box.

Ingredients:

- 1 2-3 graham cracker sandwich's with chocolate hazelnut spread
- 2 1/3 cup garbanzo beans
- 3 5-6 broccoli and cauliflower florets
- 4 5-6 carrot/red bell pepper sticks
- 1 container ranch dressing

Instructions:

Place graham sandwich's in 1st compartment.

Place beans in 2nd compartment.

Place broccoli and cauliflower in 3rd compartment.

Place carrots and red pepper sticks in 4th compartment along with ranch dressing.

Taquito Bento Box

Mini tacos or egg rolls also make a fun box! Makes 1 bento box.

Ingredients:

- 3-5 taquitos
- 1 yogurt
- 3-5 blueberries
- 3-5 strawberries

Instructions:

Place taquitos in 1st compartment.

Place yogurt in 2nd compartment.

Place blueberries in 3rd compartment.

Place strawberries in 4th compartment.

Peanut Butter Toast and Pretzels

Try chocolate-hazelnut spread! Makes 1 bento box.

Ingredients:

- 1 1 slice peanut butter toast
- 2 5-10 pretzels
- 3 1/3 cup goldfish
- 4 1 string cheese

Instructions:

Place peanut butter toast in 1st compartment.

Place pretzels in 2nd compartment.

Place string cheese in 3rd compartment.

Place goldfish in 4th compartment.

Cut fun shapes out of the toast: or, draw fun figures into the peanut butter!

PBA

Peanut butter is a great source of protein! Makes 1 bento box.

Ingredients:

- 1 3 apple slices topped peanut butter
- ¼ cup mini marshmallows
- 2 3-5 cheese cubes or string cheese
- 3 ½ banana
- 4 3 graham crackers

Instructions:

Smear peanut butter on apple slices, place mini marshmallows upright in peanut butter, and place in 1st compartment.

Place cheese cubes in 2nd compartment.

Place ½ banana in 3rd compartment.

Place graham crackers in 4th compartment.

Casual Friday Bento

Don't forget the ketchup! Makes 1 bento box.

Ingredients:

- 3-4 chicken nuggets
- 1 pudding pack
- 1 box raisins
- 2-3 sandwich cookies

Instructions:

Place nuggets and ketchup in 1st compartment.

Place pudding in 2nd compartment.

Place raisins in 3rd compartment.

Place cookies in 4th compartment.

Slider Bento Box

Veggie burgers/bean burgers work too! Makes 1 bento box.

Ingredients:

- 1-2 slider buns
- 1-2 slider hamburger patty
- Mayonnaise
- 5-8 French fries or tater tots
- 4-5 veggie chips
- 2-4 slices of pineapple

Instructions:

Layout bread, spread on mayonnaise, top with slider, then put in first compartment.

Place fries/tots in 2nd compartment.

Place veggie chips in 3rd compartment.

Place pineapple slices in 4th compartment.

Pizza Bagel Bento Box

Try pizza rolls. Makes 1 bento box.

Ingredients:

- 2-3 pizza bagels such as Bagel Bites
- 5-6 goldfish
- 1/3 cup worth sliced strawberries
- 2-3 chocolate sandwich cookies such as Oreo's

Instructions:

Wrap warm bagels in aluminum foil or airtight container. If not kept in insulated container the bagels will lose their structural integrity and the cheese gets rubbery. Place in 1st compartment.

Place goldfish in 2nd compartment.

Place strawberries in 3rd compartment.

Place cookies in 4th compartment.

Fajita Bento

Use up those leftovers! Makes 1 bento box.

Ingredients:

- 1/2 cup shredded chicken meat
- 1/3 tsp chili powder
- 3 bell pepper sticks, halved
- 1/3 cup shredded cheddar cheese or Mexican blend cheese
- ¼ cup rice
- ¼ cup corn
- 3-5 tortilla chips

Instructions:

Mix shredded chicken, chili powder, pepper halves, cheese. Re-warm, place in insulated box, then place in 1st compartment.

Place rice in 2nd compartment.

Place corn in 3rd compartment.

Place tortilla chips in 4th compartment.

B.L.T. Bento Box

Substitute the carrots with mini corn! Makes 1 bento box.

Ingredients:

- 1 bacon, lettuce, and tomato sandwich cut into 4 squares
- 1/4 cup black beans
- 5 roasted carrots
- 5 roasted beans

Instructions:

Place B.L.T. squares in 1st compartment.

Place black beans in 2nd compartment.

Place carrots in 3rd compartment.

Place beans in 4th compartment.

Grill Cheese and Graham Crackers

Grill cheeses are great with herbs! Makes 1 bento box.

Ingredients:

- 1 grill cheese cut into 4 squares
- 1/4 cup squares cereal (examples: Chex Shredded Wheat)
- 5-8 mini marshmallows
- 2-3 graham cracker sandwich's made with chocolate-hazelnut spread

Instructions:

Place grill cheese squares in 1st compartment.

Place cereal in 2nd compartment.

Place marshmallows in 3rd compartment.

Place graham cracker sandwich's in 4th compartment.

Taco Salad Bento Box

If desired, throw in some lettuce and tomato! Makes 1 bento box.

Ingredients:

- 1 cup leftover taco ground beef
- ¼ cup shredded cheese
- 1/3 cup whole kernel corn
- 5-8 corn chips
- 3-4 cookies

Instructions:

Mix taco meat and shredded cheese and place in 1st compartment.

Place corn in 2nd compartment.

Place corn chips in 3rd compartment.

Place cookies in 4th compartment.

Fish Sticks and Spirals

Substitute ½ of a banana for the bell pepper sticks! Makes 1 bento box.

Ingredients:

- 4-5 fish sticks
- 1/2 cup sweet potato spirals
- 5 bell pepper sticks
- 1 pack small chocolate candies (such as MMS)

Instructions:

Place fish sticks in 1st compartment.

Place spirals in 2nd compartment.

Place pepper sticks in 3rd compartment.

Place candies in 4th compartment.

Turkey Wrap Bento Box

Try this wrap as a pita!! Makes 1 bento box.

Ingredients:

- 1 turkey wrap, halved
- ¼ cup goldfish
- 1 yogurt
- 1 blondie brownie

Instructions:

Place both halves of turkey wrap in 1st compartment.

Place goldfish in 2nd compartment.

Place yogurt in 3rd compartment.

Place brownie in 4th compartment.

Sweet Sour Chicken Strip Bento

Leftover pork medallions work too! Makes 1 bento box.

Ingredients:

- 3 chicken strips
- 1 container of sweet and sour sauce
- 4-5 pieces bok choy
- 1 fortune cookie
- 5-10 rice crackers

Instructions:

Wrap warm chicken strips in foil and place in 1st compartment.

Place bok choy pieces in 2nd compartment.

Place fortune cookie in 3rd compartment.

Place crackers in 4th compartment.

Pasta Salad Bento Box

Try all the pasta shapes! Makes 1 bento box.

Ingredients:

- 2/3 cup corkscrew macaroni
- 2-3 grape tomatoes, halved
- 3-4 broccoli pieces
- 1 container Italian dressing
- ½ chocolate bar

Instructions:

Make macaroni as directed then place in 1st compartment.

Place container of Italian dressing in with noodles.

Place tomatoes in 2nd compartment.

Place broccoli pieces in 3rd compartment.

Place ½ of chocolate bar in 4th compartment.

Blueberry Dollars

For casual days, try chocolate chip pancakes! Makes 1 bento box.

Ingredients:

- 2-3 silver dollar blueberry pancakes
- 1/3 cup banana chips
- 1 container cinnamon applesauce
- Blueberry yogurt

Instructions:

Place pancakes in 1st compartment.

Place banana chips in 2nd compartment.

Place container of applesauce in 3rd compartment.

Place blueberry yogurt in 4th compartment.

Ham Turkey Rolls

A great box for quick protein! Makes 1 bento box.

Ingredients:

- 1-2 slices of ham
- 1-2 slices of turkey
- 2-4 slices of provolone or mozzarella cheese
- 2-3 whole strawberries
- 3-4 blueberries
- 1 brownie

Instructions:

Roll all ham and turkey slices in cheese and place in 1st compartment.

Place strawberries in 2nd compartment.

Place strawberries and blueberries in 3rd compartment.

Place brownie in 4th compartment.

Starry P.B J Bento

Substitute the cheese with garbanzo beans! Makes 1 bento box.

Ingredients:

- 1 star shaped peanut butter and jelly sandwich
- 1/4 cup goldfish
- 4-5 cheese cubes
- 1 box raisins or cranberries

Instructions:

Place star shaped sandwich in 1st compartment.

Place goldfish in 2nd compartment.

Place cheese cubes in 3rd compartment.

Place raisins in 4th compartment.

P.B. Muffins Beans

Or, blueberry or strawberry organic muffins! Makes 1 bento box.

Ingredients:

- 5 seedless grapes
- 1 avocado, diced
- ¼ cup garbanzo beans
- 2 peanut butter jam muffins

Instructions:

Place grapes in 1st compartment.

Place diced avocados in 2nd compartment.

Place cherry tomatoes in 3rd compartment.

Place muffins in 4th compartment.

Pizza Rolls Apple Slices

Another great protein box for casual days! Makes 1 bento box.

Ingredients:

- 5 crackers
- 5-8 goldfish
- 5-8 apple slices
- 3-6 pepperoni pizza rolls

Instructions:

Place crackers in 1st compartment.

Place goldfish in 2nd compartment.

Place apple slices in 3rd compartment.

Place pizza rolls in 4th compartment.

Author's Afterthoughts

Thanks ever so much to each of my cherished readers for investing the time to read this book!

I know you could have picked from many other books, but you chose this one. So, a big thanks for reading all the way to the end. If you enjoyed this book or received value from it, I'd like to ask you for a favor. Please take a few minutes to *post an honest and heartfelt review on Amazon.com.* Your support does make a difference and helps to benefit other people.

Thanks!

Julia Chiles

About the Author

Julia Chiles

(1951-present)

Julia received her culinary degree from Le Counte' School of Culinary Delights in Paris, France. She enjoyed cooking more than any of her former positions. She lived in Montgomery, Alabama most of her life. She married Roger

Chiles and moved with him to Paris as he pursued his career in journalism. During the time she was there, she joined several cooking groups to learn the French cuisine, which inspired her to attend school and become a great chef.

Julia has achieved many awards in the field of food preparation. She has taught at several different culinary schools. She is in high demand on the talk show circulation, sharing her knowledge and recipes. Julia's favorite pastime is learning new ways to cook old dishes.

Julia is now writing cookbooks to add to her long list of achievements. The present one consists of favorite recipes as well as a few culinary delights from other cultures. She expands everyone's expectations on how to achieve wonderful dishes and not spend a lot of money. Julia firmly believes a wonderful dish can be prepare out of common household staples.

If anyone is interested in collecting Julia's cookbooks, check out your local bookstores and online. They are a big seller whatever venue you choose to purchase from.